An unfinished man

by Dipo Baruwa-Etti

An unfinished man was produced by and first
performed at The Yard Theatre, London,
on 12 February 2022

An unfinished man

Dipo Baruwa-Etti

Cast

Kayode	Fode Simbo
Kikiope	Teri Ann Bobb-Baxter
Layo	Lucy Vandi
Matanmi	Mark Springer
Itan	Selina Jones

Creative Team

Writer	Dipo Baruwa-Etti
Director	Taio Lawson
Designer	Rosie Elnile
Lighting Designer	Ciarán Cunningham
Sound Designer	George Dennis
Movement Director	Robia Milliner
Fight Director	Yarit Dor
Casting Director	Briony Barnett
Assistant Director	Garen Abel Unokan
Costume Supervisor	Rianna Azoro
Production Dramatherapist	Wabriya King
Production Manager	Tammy Rose
Company Stage Manager	Julia Nimmo
Assistant Stage Manager	Farideh Didehvar

Cast and Creative Team

Fode Simbo (KAYODE)
Fode Simbo trained at Guildhall School of Acting. Theatre credits include: *Solaris* (Royal Lyceum Theatre/Lyric Hammersmith), *Princess & The Hustler* (Bristol Old Vic), *Young Marx* (Bridge Theatre). Film credits include: *Fisherman's Friends 2*. Television credits include: *Vigil, Summer of Rockets, Little Women*.

Teri Ann Bobb-Baxter (KIKIOPE)
Teri Ann Bobb-Baxter trained at the Arts Educational School in London where she completed her BA in Acting. She also attended the BRIT School for Performing Arts, training in Musical Theatre. Theatre credits include: *Ma Rainey's Black Bottom* (National Theatre), *Future Voices* (Southwark Playhouse), *Expensive Sh*** (Traverse Theatre). Television credits include: *Call the Midwife, War of the Worlds, Bridgerton, Clink, Hard Sun*.

Lucy Vandi (LAYO)
Lucy Vandi trained at Mountview. She previously appeared at The Yard Theatre in *The Crucible*. Theatre credits include: *Tina: The Tina Turner Musical* (Aldwych Theatre), *How Far Apart?* (Arcola Theatre), *The Midnight Gang* (Chichester Festival Theatre), *Hoard* (Bush Theatre), *Guys & Dolls* (Royal Exchange Theatre), *School of Rock* (Gillian Lynne Theatre), *Ma Rainey's Black Bottom, The Life of Galileo, Jerry Springer: The Opera* (National Theatre), *The Last Session* (Tristan Bates Theatre), *The Lion, the Witch and the Wardrobe* (Leicester Haymarket Theatre). Television credits include: *Casualty, EastEnders, Doctors, Mile High* (BBC), *Bridgerton* (Netflix).

Mark Springer (MATANMI)
Mark Springer trained at Manchester Metropolitan School of Television & Theatre. Theatre credits include: *Sing Yer Heart Out for the Lads* (Chichester Festival Theatre), *The Island* (The Dukes, Southwark Playhouse), *Henry V, Troilus and Cressida, The Merchant of Venice, The Darker Face of the Earth* (National Theatre), *Thomas More, A New Way To Please You, Believe What You Will* (Royal Shakespeare Company), *Macbeth, Much Ado About Nothing, Romeo and Juliet* (Shakespeare's Globe), *Don Juan* (Citizens Theatre), *King Lear* (Royal Exchange Theatre, Talawa Theatre Company), *The Emperor Jones* (LOST Theatre), *Chigger Foot Boys* (Ovalhouse, Strongback Productions), *Meet the Mukherjees* (Octagon Theatre), *Where the Mangrove Grows, Songs of Grace and Redemption* (Theatre503), *The Chimes* (Southwark Playhouse), *The Suppliants* (Gate Theatre), *A Taste of*

Honey (Watford Palace Theatre), *Night and Day* (Royal & Derngate). Television credits include: *Shadow and Bone*, *One Night*, *Buried* (BAFTA Best Drama), *New Tricks*, *Doctor Who*, *Sea of Souls*, *Eastenders*, *Holby City*, *Law & Order* (UK), *Rose and Maloney*, *In Two Minds*, *Merchant of Venice*, *Doctors*, *Second Generation*, *The Bill*. Film credits include: *Kingslayer*, *Bull*, *King Lear* (Royal Exchange Theatre, Talawa Theatre Company), *Sahara* (Paramount Pictures), *Acceptable Damage* (Rebel Without A Crew).

Selina Jones (ITAN)
Selina Jones trained at LAMDA. She recently shot the highly anticipated second season of Ridley Scott's *Raised by Wolves* for HBO Max. The series is due to air in February 2022 where Selina can be seen playing the role of 'Grandmother'. Selina recently played one of the lead roles in the short film *Nadia's Gift* and starred in another short, *Medea*, playing the title role. Theatre credits include: *Nine Night*, *The Winter's Tale*, *The Wolves*, *The Seagull* (LAMDA).

Dipo Baruwa-Etti (Writer)
Dipo Baruwa-Etti is a filmmaker, playwright and poet. As a playwright, Dipo was the 2020 Channel 4 Playwright on attachment with the Almeida Theatre and was shortlisted for the George Devine Most Promising Playwright Award that same year. As a poet, he has been published in *The Good Journal*, *Ink Sweat & Tears*, *Amaryllis*, and had his work showcased nationwide as part of End Hunger UK's touring exhibition on food insecurity. For screen, he wrote and directed the award-winning short film *The Last Days* (BFI Network/BBC/Tannahill Productions) and has original projects in development with companies including Blueprint Pictures and Duck Soup Films. Theatre credits include: *The Sun, the Moon, and the Stars* (Theatre Royal Stratford East), and he is published by Faber & Faber.

Taio Lawson (Director)
Taio Lawson was most recently the Associate Director of Kiln Theatre. Prior to this role Taio was Resident Director at Sheffield Theatres where he collaborated on *Love and Information*, *Frost/Nixon*, *The Wizard of Oz* and *Desire Under The Elms*. Director credits include: *NW Stories* (Kiln Theatre), *HOME Digital* (Young Vic Theatre), *Macbeth* (Royal Conservatoire of Scotland), *Hang* (Crucible Theatre), *White Devil* (East 15 Acting School), *Home – Installation* (Young Vic Theatre), *How To Make Love To A Muslim Without Freaking Out* (Rehearsed Reading, Bush Theatre), *Face in a Jar* (St Paul's Furzedown Church/Rhoda McGaw

Theatre), *What We Are*, *90s Kid* (Etcetera Theatre), *Gutted 'n' Battered* (UK/international tour), *Sexy Buff Ting* (The Cockpit). Assistant Director credits include: *Life of Galileo*, *Sizwe Banzi Is Dead* (Young Vic Theatre), *Oil*, *They Drink It in the Congo* (Almeida Theatre), *Octagon* (Arcola Theatre), *Perseverance Drive* (Bush Theatre). Taio is also a patron for COMMON which is a non-profit arts organisation which exists to support the UK theatre industry in achieving greater socio-economic diversity, and make theatre more accessible to the working class; whether they be artists, audiences or communities.

Rosie Elnile (Designer)
Rosie Elnile is a performance designer and artist based between the UK and Portugal. She was a recipient of the 2020 Jerwood Live Art Fund. Theatre includes: *A Fight Against*, *Goats* (Royal Court Theatre), *Peaceaphobia* (Fuel Theatre/Common Wealth Theatre), *Prayer*, *The Ridiculous Darkness*, *Unknown Island*, *The Convert* (Gate Theatre), *Thirst Trap* (Fuel Theatre), *Run Sister Run* (Crucible Theatre), *[Blank]* (Donmar Warehouse), *Our Town* (Regent's Park Open Air Theatre), *The American Clock* (The Old Vic), *The Wolves* (Theatre Royal Stratford East), *The Mysteries*, *Three Sisters* (Royal Exchange Theatre), *Abandon* (Lyric Hammersmith), *Returning to Haifa* (Finborough Theatre), *BIG GUNS* (The Yard Theatre).

Ciarán Cunningham (Lighting Designer)
Ciarán Cunningham trained at East 15 Acting School. Lighting design credits include: *Freedom Project* (Leeds Playhouse), *Me for the World* (Young Vic Theatre), *Amsterdam* (Orange Tree Theatre/UK tour), *Blood Knot* (Orange Tree Theatre), *One Night In Miami* (Nottingham Playhouse/Bristol Old Vic/HOME Manchester), *Suckerpunch Boom Suite* (Barbican Centre/nitroBEAT), *Eden* (Hampstead Theatre), *Sleeping Beauty* (Theatre Royal Stratford East), *Shebeen* (Nottingham Playhouse/Theatre Royal Stratford East), *Last Days of Iscariot* (Vanbrugh Theatre), *Dublin Carol* (Sherman Theatre), *Into the Woods*, *Brink* (Royal Exchange Theatre), *Wish List* (Royal Exchange Theatre/Royal Court Theatre), *Sizwe Banzi Is Dead* (Young Vic Theatre/UK tour), *Sound of Yellow* (Young Vic Theatre), *Sense of Sound: Migration Music* (Everyman Theatre), *Scrappers* (Liverpool Playhouse Theatre), *In His Hands; Re:Definition* (Hackney Empire), *Blackout* (The Dukes), *The Mountaintop* (Welsh national tour), *Death and the Maiden* (The Other Room), *A Dream Across the Ocean* (Ashcroft Theatre), *When Chaplin Met Gandhi* (Kingsley Hall), *Normal* (RIFT), *Chris Dugdale: 2 Faced Deception* (Leicester Square Theatre), *Letter to Larry* (Jermyn Street Theatre).

George Dennis (Sound Designer)
George Dennis studied at Manchester University. He received an Olivier Award nomination for Best Sound Design in 2016 for *The Homecoming* and, with Ben and Max Ringham, won the 2018 Off-West End Award for Best Sound Design for *Killer*. Theatre credits include: *The Homecoming* (Trafalgar Theatre), *A Slight Ache & The Dumb Waiter*, *The Lover & The Collection*, *One for the Road*, *A New World Order*, *Mountain Language & Ashes to Ashes* (Harold Pinter Theatre), *Nine Night* (National Theatre/Trafalgar Theatre), *An Octoroon* (Orange Tree Theatre/National Theatre), *Sweat* (Donmar Warehouse/Gielgud Theatre), *The Importance of Being Earnest* (Vaudeville Theatre), *The Windsors: Endgame* (Prince of Wales Theatre), *Glee & Me* (Royal Exchange Theatre), *The Duchess of Malfi*, *Three Sisters* (Almeida Theatre), *Venice Preserved* (Royal Shakespeare Company), *Talent*, *Frost/Nixon*, *Tribes* (Crucible Theatre), *The Mountaintop* (Young Vic Theatre/Royal Exchange Theatre/UK tour), *Sing Yer Heart Out for the Lads*, *The Deep Blue Sea*, *The Norman Conquests* (Chichester Festival Theatre), *Two Ladies*, *A Very Very Very Dark Matter* (Bridge Theatre), *The Beacon* (Staatstheater Stuttgart), *Hedda Tesman*, *Richard III*, *Spring Awakening* (Headlong Theatre), *The Island* (Young Vic Theatre), *Much Ado About Nothing*, *Imogen*, *The Taming of the Shrew* (Shakespeare's Globe), *Harrogate*, *Fireworks*, *Liberian Girl* (Royal Court Theatre), *Guards at the Taj*, *Visitors* (Bush Theatre), *Killer*, *The Pitchfork Disney* (Shoreditch Town Hall, co-designed with Ben and Max Ringham), *Faces in the Crowd*, *The Convert*, *In the Night Time*, *Eclipsed* (Gate Theatre).

Robia Milliner (Movement Director)
Robia Milliner has trained at the Brit School, her choreography is a blend of Hip-Hop, Contemporary and Jazz. One style becomes more prominent depending on where a particular piece of music takes her. Robia has been performing, choreographing and teaching in London for over ten years. She has worked with companies and choreographers such as Still House Dance Company, Hofesh Schecter and Ivan Blackstock, as well as creating much work as a solo artist. She has taught masterclasses globally sharing her vast knowledge with students from Japan to Europe. Over the past few years, she has taken a big interest in Movement Directing, where she is now rehearsal director for FUBU Nation and assisting more in the commercial dance scene with the likes of Beyoncé and Rita Ora, as well as the theatre industry on *Message In A Bottle* and *Hymn*.

Yarit Dor (Fight Director)
Yarit Dor is an established fight director, movement director, intimacy coordinator and credited as the first intimacy director in the West End, London, UK. She is co-director of Moving Body Arts and Ensemble Associate Artist of Shakespeare's Globe. Theatre credits include: *Dirty Crusty*, *The Crucible* (The Yard Theatre), *Rockets and Blue Lights* (National Theatre), *The Shark is Broken* (Ambassadors Theatre), *Death of a Salesman* (Piccadilly Theatre/Young Vic Theatre), *Love and Other Acts of Violence* (Donmar Warehouse), *Richard II*, *Hamlet*, *As You Like It*, *Much Ado About Nothing* (Shakespeare's Globe), *NW Trilogy* (Kiln Theatre), *Changing Destiny*, *Wild East* (Young Vic Theatre), *Daddy* (Almeida Theatre), *Macbeth* (Royal Exchange Theatre), *Statements After an Arrest Under the Immorality Act*, *Last Easter* (Orange Tree Theatre), *Miss Julie* (Storyhouse), *Assata Taught Me* (Gate Theatre), *The Effect* (Boulevard Theatre), *Romeo and Juliet*, *As You Like It*, *A Midsummer Night's Dream* (Shakespeare in the Squares), *Little Voice*, *Disgraced* (Park Theatre), *Titus Andronicus* (Greenwich Theatre). Dance includes: *Rooms* (Rambert Dance Company), *Between A Self And An Other*, *Leah*, *2B*, *Sunday Morning* (Hagit Yakira Company). Film includes: *The Colour Room*, *Knives Out 2*, *Polite Society*. Television includes: *The Wheel of Time*, *Adult Material*, *Atlanta 3*, *Superhoe*, *The Girlfriend Experience 3*, *Pistol*, *Close To Me*, *Spanish Princess 2*, *Becoming Elizabeth*, *Domina*, *White Lines*, *Starstruck*, and more.

Briony Barnett CDG (Casting Director)
Theatre credits include: *The Memory of Water*, *The Death of a Black Man* (Hampstead Theatre), *Overflow*, *Chiaroscuro*, *An Adventure* (Bush Theatre), *NW Trilogy*, *The Invisible Hand*, *When the Crows Visit*, *White Teeth* (Kiln Theatre), *Princess & The Hustler* (Bristol Old Vic/tour), *Half God of Rainfall* (Kiln Theatre/Birmingham Repertory Theatre), *Black Men Walking* (Scottish tour), *The Trick* (Bush Theatre/tour), *Again* (West End), *Abigail's Party* (Hull Truck Theatre), *Black Men Walking* (Royal Exchange Theatre/tour), *Handbagged* (Vaudeville Theatre/Tricycle Theatre), *Fences* (Duchess Theatre/Theatre Royal Bath), *A Raisin in the Sun* (Crucible Theatre/tour), *Ticking* (Trafalgar Theatre), *Play Mas* (Orange Tree Theatre), *Chasing Rainbows*, *Female Parts* (Hoxton Hall), *Ben Hur*, *A Wolf in Snakeskin Shoes*, *The House That Will Not Stand*, *The Colby Sisters*, *One Monkey Don't Stop No Show* (Tricycle Theatre). Film credits include: *Bluebird*, *Samuel's Trousers*, *Bruce*, *Gypsy's Kiss*, *The Knot*, *High Tide*, *What We Did On Our Holiday* (children), *Common People*, *Tezz*, *Final Prayer*, *Love/Loss*, *Zero Sum*, *Travellers*, *Janet and Bernard*, *Stop*, *A Sunny Morning*, *Value Life*, *Conversation Piece*, *10by10*.

Television credits include: *Outnumbered* (children), *Just Around the Corner* (children), *Dickensian* (children), *Inside the Mind of Leonardo*.

Garen Abel Unokan (Assistant Director)
Garen Abel Unokan was the Assistant Director on *Jacaranda* by Lorna French and directed by Elle While, a Pentabus and Theatre by the Lake co-production (2021). She was also the Young Vic Theatre's Boris Karloff Trainee Assistant Director in 2018, supported by the Boris Karloff Foundation on *The Convert* by Danai Gurira and directed by Ola Ince. Garen's writing has appeared in publications such as *The New Yorker* and *Black Ballad*, and she is currently working on her first novel. As an artist, Garen is particularly interested in narratives surrounding queerness, blackness, coming of age, and autonomy. Theatre credits include: *lovesexidentityambition* (Theatre503, 2020), *Can I Touch Your Hair?* (VAULT Festival, 2019), *Glutathione* (Replay: Young Vic Theatre, 2019), *Blend.Share.Mix* (Rapid Write Response at Theatre503, 2019).

Rianna Azoro (Costume Supervisor)
Rianna Azoro is a Costume Supervisor and Designer from South London who started out by completing a Costume Apprenticeship at the Young Vic Theatre in 2016. Theatre credits include, as Costume Designer: *Girls* (New Diorama Theatre). As Costume Supervisor: *A Number* (The Old Vic), *Seven Methods of Killing Kylie Jenner* (Royal Court Theatre), *The Half God of Rainfall* (Kiln Theatre/Birmingham Repertory Theatre), *Nine Night* (Trafalgar Theatre), *Richard II* (Shakespeare's Globe), *The Mountaintop* (Young Vic Theatre), *Strange Fruit* (Bush Theatre). TV credits include: *Smothered* (Sky), *So Beano* (Sky), *Great British Bake Off* (Love productions). Other work includes: 'Fever', music video by Dua Lipa & Angèle (Iconoclast).

Wabriya King (Production Dramatherapist)
Wabriya graduated as an actress from the Oxford School of Drama in 2012 and qualified with an MA in Dramatherapy from the University of Roehampton in 2019. She believes that the arts have a responsibility to its performers to support their mental health wellbeing. This is clearly a shared belief as, as her work is gaining momentum within theatre and screen. Wabriya recently became the Associate Dramatherapist at the Bush Theatre supporting staff and productions, including: *Old Bridge*, *10 Nights*, *Overflow*, *Pink Lemonade* and *Lava*. Separate to the Bush Theatre, Wabriya worked alongside: *Rockets and Blue Lights* (National Theatre), *Can I Live?* (Complicité), *Get Up, Stand Up!*

The Bob Marley Musical (Lyric Theatre), *White Noise* (Bridge Theatre), *Is God Is*, *Seven Methods of Killing Kylie Jenner* (Royal Court Theatre), *Curious*, *Shuck 'n' Jive*, *TYPICAL* (Soho Theatre), *For Black Boys...* (New Diorama Theatre), *Love and Other Acts of Violence* (Donmar Warehouse), *Blue/Orange* (Royal & Derngate), *Romeo and Juliet* (Shakespeare's Globe), *The Death of a Black Man* (Hampstead Theatre), *Sessions*, *May Queen*, *Black Love* (Paines Plough), *846 Live* (Theatre Royal Stratford East), *The High Table* (Bush Theatre).

Tammy Rose (Production Manager)
Theatre credits includes: *Fantastically Great Women Who Changed the World* (Kenny Wax Family Entertainment), *Into the Night*, *The Red*, *Hound of the Baskervilles*, *A Splinter of Ice*, *Being Mr Wickham*, *Cold Super Behind Harrods*, *Habit of Art*, *The Croft*, *Monogamy* (Original Theatre Company), *Looking Good Dead*, *House on Cold Hill*, *Not Dead Enough*, *Dead Simple*, *Perfect Murder* (Josh Andrews Productions), *Jina and the STEM Sisters* (HMDT), *Scarlet*, *Diminished*, *No One Will Tell Me How to Start a Revolution*, *The Firm*, *Yous Two*, *Acceptance*, *The Phlebotomist*, *The Strange Death of John Doe* (Hampstead Theatre), *The Ridiculous Darkness*, *Mephestio* (Gate Theatre), *Jack!*, *The Owl and the Pussy Cat* (Full House Productions), *Robin Hood*, *My Mother Said I Never Should*, *Mother Goose* (The Theatre Chipping Norton), *Alice in Wonderland*, *King Lear*, *The Canterbury Tales* (Guildford Shakespeare Company Trust), *The Lone Pine Club*, *Our Land*, *Here I Belong*, *As the Crow Flies*, *Wolves Are Coming For You* (Pentabus Theatre Co), *Three Tales Opera* (IMAX), *Lady Anna*, *Toast* (Park Theatre), *Clarion*, *Shrapnel: 34 Fragments of a Massacre*, *Happy Endings*, *Eldorado* (Arcola Theatre) *Brundibar*, *The Rattler* (Mahogany Opera), *The Little Green Swallow* (Peacock Theatre), *Last Days of Limehouse* (Limehouse Town Hall), *Donkey Heart* (Old Red Lion/Trafalgar Theatre), *The A–Z of Mrs P* (Southwark Playhouse), *Evita* (European tour), *Black Coffee*, *Aladdin*, *Witness for the Prosecution*, *Murder on Air*, *Grass is Greener*, *Pack of Lies* (Theatre Royal Windsor/tour), *Chin Chin*, *Fallen Angels*, *Laughter in the Rain*, *A Daughter's a Daughter*, *Dreamboats and Petticoats*, *Whistle Down the Wind* (Bill Kenwright Ltd), *Eugenie Grande* (Assembly Rooms Theatre), *Woody Sez* (UK Arts), *Cinderella* (Grimaldi Forum).

Julia Nimmo (Company Stage Manager)
Julia Nimmo trained in Design for Theatre & Television at Charles Stuart University, Wagga Wagga, Australia and was awarded 'Individual Stage Manager of the Year' at the SMA National Stage Manager awards 2019. Stage Manager theatre credits include:

Run It Back (Talawa Theatre Company), *Buffering...* (Watford Palace Theatre, Palace Youth Company), *Queer Lives* (Historic Royal Palaces, Tower of London), *Pepper & Honey* (Notnow Collective), *Rust*, *The Trick* (HighTide Theatre/Bush Theatre), *The Witches* (Watford Palace Theatre, Herfordshire Youth Theatre Company), *Songlines* (HighTide Theatre/DugOut Theatre), *Paper. Scissors. Stone.* (Tara Finney Productions Ltd), *Frankie Vah* (Paul Jellis Ltd), *All the Things I Lied About* (Paul Jellis Ltd/Katie Bonna), *Harrogate* (HighTide Theatre/Royal Court Theatre), *This Much* (Moving Dust), *Flare Path* (Birdsong Productions/Original Theatre Company), *Lampedusa* (HighTide Theatre/Soho Theatre), *Beached* (Marlowe Theatre/Soho Theatre), *The One* (Soho Theatre), *The Real Thing* (English Touring Theatre), *Macbeth* (Wildfire Productions, Cell Block Theatre), *The Beauty Queen of Leenane* (Wildfire Productions, Seymour Centre, Sydney). Festival credits include: Wow Festival (Hull 2017), Talawa First Festival (2017 & 2018).

Farideh Didehvar (Assistant Stage Manager)
Farideh Didehvar was born in 1998, in Mashhad, Iran. She received her Bachelor's degree in English Language and Literature from Ferdowsi University of Mashhad. During her undergraduate studies, she joined, and later became a member of the central board of, a student-run theatre organisation, where she trained to write, act and direct. It was in this society where she wrote and directed her first plays, and decided to choose the field of theatre and performance for her future studies. She recently graduated from Goldsmiths, University of London, in Performance Making MA and she has been doing different projects and working in different capacities ever since.

Supporter Credits

This production of *An unfinished man* was developed with support from Arts Council England, The London Community Foundation, Cockayne Grants for the Arts, Unity Theatre Trust, and the Culture Recovery Fund from DCMS and Arts Council England.

The Yard would like to extend additional thanks to The Idlewild Trust for their generous support to Dipo via Yard New Voices, which supported artists to develop their first full commissions.

Thanks

Thank you to everyone who helped us make *An unfinished man*. We couldn't have done it without you.

The team who made the show would like to thank: Martha Amara, Lekan Babalola, Gate Theatre, Dan Gosselin, Grantham Hazeldine Agents, Karley Hewitt, John Hyslop, Wil Johnson, Christopher James Jones, Yeama Kamara, Tife Kusoro, Anthony Lennon, Mimi Ndiweni, Pamela Nomvete, Vivian Oparah, Theo Ogundipe, Yetunde Oduwole, Pure Garden Buildings, Sarah Roberts, Elise Tchameni, Shelley Williams

The Yard Theatre

'*The future has arrived in Hackney Wick in the form of The Yard*' Lyn Gardner, *Guardian*

The Yard is a theatre and music venue in a converted warehouse in Hackney Wick.

The Yard was founded by Artistic Director Jay Miller in 2011, with support from Tarek Iskander, Sasha Milavic Davies and Alex Rennie and a group of 50 volunteers. They worked with architectural firm Practice Architecture to convert a disused warehouse into a theatre and bar.

The Yard is at the centre of its community, reaching thousands of local people every year through programmes in local schools and in the community centres the theatre runs: Hub67 in Hackney Wick and The Hall in East Village. These programmes include creative projects for young people aged 4-19 years, and regular activities for local people.

The Yard is also one of London's most exciting venues for experiencing music, welcoming parties by and for under-represented groups in London's nightlife scene, supporting artists who make music or performance for bars and club spaces, as well as hosting internationally renowned DJs and promoters.

Since 2011 The Yard's programme has been seen by hundreds of thousands of people, and shows have have transferred to the National Theatre, been turned into television series and toured the UK.

Recent productions include:

Athena written by Grace Gummer, directed by Grace Gardner ★★★★ *The Stage*

Dirty Crusty written by Clare Barron, directed by Jay Miller ★★★★★ *Evening Standard*

Armadillo written by Sarah Kosar, directed by Sara Joyce ★★★★ *WhatsOnStage*

The Crucible written by Arthur Miller, directed by Jay Miller ★★★★★ *Evening Standard*

A New and Better You written by Joe Harbot, directed by Cheryl Gallacher ★★★★ *Guardian*

Buggy Baby written by Josh Azouz, directed by Ned Bennett ★★★★★ *WhatsOnStage*

This Beautiful Future written by Rita Kalnejais, directed by Jay Miller ★★★★★ *The Stage*

Removal Men written by M. J. Harding, with Jay Miller ★★★★ *Time Out*

LINES written by Pamela Carter, directed by Jay Miller ★★★★ *Time Out*

The Mikvah Project written by Josh Azouz, directed by Jay Miller ★★★★ *Time Out*

Beyond Caring by Alexander Zeldin ★★★★ *Guardian*

The Yard Theatre

The Yard Supporters

Arts Council England
Bloomberg Philanthropies
Bristows LLP
Chapman Charitable Trust
Get Living London
London Legacy Development
    Corporation
Newham Council
Takero Shimazaki Architects
Taylor Wimpey
The Boris Karloff Charitable
    Trust
The Childhood Trust
The Foyle Foundation
The Garfield Weston
    Foundation
The Goldsmiths Company
The Harold Hyam Wingate
    Foundation
The Henry Smith Charity
The John Ellerman Foundation
The Kirsh Foundation
The National Lottery
    Community Fund
The Patrick and Helena Frost
    Foundation
The Ragdoll Foundation
The Sigrid Rausing Trust
Theatres Trust
Tower Hamlets Council
Wick Award

FRIENDS & GUARDIANS
Thank you to all our Friends
and Guardians including:
Mike Anderson
Rosie Beaumont-Thomas
Kelly Bewers
Francesco Curto & Chantal
    Rivest
The David Pearlman Charitable
    Foundation
Greg Delaney

Ian & Janet Edmondson
Pam & Peter Hansford
Jack Haynes
Nick Hytner
Alex Ingram
Melanie Johnson
Joanna Kennedy
Lauren McLeod
Ben Rogers
Robin Saphra
Peter Snook
Ida Stamm
Clive & Sally Sherling
Anna Vaughan & Dan Fletcher
Adam Tyndall
Archie Ward
Carolyn Ward
Garry Watts
Hyman Wolanski
Gabriel Vogt

And all our supporters who
prefer to remain anonymous

CORPORATE SUPPORTERS
Bristows LLP
Takero Shimazaki Architects

An unfinished man

Dipo Baruwa-Etti is a playwright, poet and filmmaker. In 2020, he was shortlisted for the George Devine Award and was the Channel 4 playwright on attachment at the Almeida Theatre. His debut play *The Sun, the Moon, and the Stars* premiered at Theatre Royal Stratford East and was shortlisted for the Alfred Fagon Award for Best New Play. For screen, he wrote and directed the award-winning short film *The Last Days* (BFI Network/BBC/Tannahill Productions) and has several original projects in development. As a poet, he has been published in *The Good Journal*, *Ink Sweat & Tears* and *Amaryllis*, and had his work showcased nationwide as part of End Hunger UK's touring exhibition on food insecurity.

DIPO BARUWA-ETTI

An unfinished man

faber

First published in 2022
by Faber and Faber Limited
74–77 Great Russell Street
London WC1B 3DA

Typeset by Brighton Gray
Printed and bound in the UK by CPI Group (Ltd), Croydon CR0 4YY

A CIP record for this book
is available from the British Library

978-0-571-36347-6

2 4 6 8 10 9 7 5 3 1

Acknowledgements

Thank you to God, Mum, the siblings, all my family and those who've been a part of this play's journey including:

Taio Lawson, Fode Simbo, Teri Ann Bobb-Baxter
Selina Jones, Lucy Vandi, Mark Springer

Lara Tysseling, Jay Miller, Sam Hansford
Ashleigh Wheeler, all at The Yard Theatre

Rosie Elnile, George Dennis, Ciaran Cunningham
Briony Barnett, Robia Milliner, Garen Abel Unokan
Yarit Dor, Julia Nimmo, Farideh Didehvar
Wabriya King, Rianna Azoro, Tammy Rose

Mimi M Khayisa, Theo Ogundipe, Vivian Oparah
Wil Johnson, Pamela Nomvete
all who helped voice these characters along the way

Indhu Rubasingham, Jenny Bakst, Becky Latham
Grace Gummer, Rose Cobbe, Florence Hyde
Dinah Wood, Faber, Museum of the Mind

all who gave feedback, advice
spoke to me about the play
its themes and their lives.

An unfinished man was first performed at The Yard Theatre, London, on 12 February 2022, with the following cast and creative team:

Kayode Fode Simbo
Kikiope Teri Ann Bobb-Baxter
Layo Lucy Vandi
Matanmi Mark Springer
Itan Selina Jones

Director Taio Lawson
Designer Rosie Elnile
Lighting Designer Ciarán Cunningham
Sound Designer George Dennis
Movement Director Robia Milliner
Fight Director Yarit Dor
Casting Director Briony Barnett
Assistant Director Garen Abel Unokan
Costume Supervisor Rianna Azoro
Production Dramatherapist Wabriya King
Production Manager Tammy Rose
Company Stage Manager Julia Nimmo
Assistant Stage Manager Farideh Didehvar

Characters

Kayode
late twenties, male

Kikiope
late twenties, female

Layo
fifties, female

Matanmi
fifties, male

Itan
same age as Kayode, female

They are all Black

Setting

East London, today

AN UNFINISHED MAN

Note

Kayode and Itan often speak to each other in Shukabhembemese – a fictional language spoken and understood by only the two of them. Translations can be found at the end of the play.

The action takes place in various locations. However, throughout Kayode stands in an ocean with everyone else on the shore – never crossing over.

Except Itan, who does as she pleases.

*

A dash at the end of a word or line indicates speech interrupted by the following line.

A dash on its own line indicates a pause. The number of these in a row suggests the duration of the pause, but these can be altered, as directors feel appropriate.

Character names underneath each other without a space indicate two or more characters speaking simultaneously.

Dialogue in bold is directly to the audience. Only Itan does this.

Stage directions are in italics and right-aligned.

Prologue

In front of an ocean,
Kayode and Kikiope stand,
Itan lingering nearby.

'By Your Side' by Sade plays
as past conversations
replay, which we hear
via voice-over.

Kikiope Kayode

Kayode yh

Kikiope You alright?

Kayode yh

Kikiope Good.

–

How was swimmin?

Kayode woke up late
  i'll go next week

Kikiope D'you go on your walk?

Kayode barking road an' back

Kikiope How'd it feel?

Another conversation
(in italics) begins simultaneously.

Kikiope *(playfully)* What're you doin?
Kayode gd

13

Kikiope Good.
Kayode *Haven't you ever wanted to dance in the rain?*

Kikiope *Kayode, my hair.*

Kayode *Who cares? You've got me an' Sade.*

Kikiope *Sade ain't enough to get me drenched.*

Kayode *What bout me?*
Kikiope You ain't dressed.

Kayode *Will you dance in the rain with me?*
Kikiope Thought we were goin to –

Kayode I can't do this any more.

Kikiope Do what?

Kayode I can't –

> *Kayode steps into the ocean.*
> *He stays there throughout the play,*
> *everyone else on the shore*
> *(except Itan, who goes*
> *wherever she pleases).*
>
> *A phone rings.*
> *Kikiope answers it.*

Kikiope Hey, I know we're late, I'm sorry.
We, erm . . .
Kayode ain't feelin too good.
We're gonna have to skip, if thass fine?

–

I'm so sorry, hun,
it's juss.
I think we need a quiet night in.
We'll try an' make it next time though
if we ain't got three strikes already.

> *She forces a chuckle.*

Thanks.
　　He juss . . .
　　He ain't . . .

Kayode *Will you dance in the rain with me?*

Kikiope No.
　　He'll be fine.
　　It's nothin.
　　He juss needs sum rest.

She hangs up.

Always.

ONE

*Kayode and Kikiope
are in their sitting room
with Matanmi.*

Itan is also present.

Kayode I don't –

Matanmi It's fine.

Kayode It ain't FINE.

Matanmi We can –
Kayode Thass crazy.

Kikiope Kayode, thass why he's here.

Matanmi Exactly.

Kayode What can you do bout it?
Matanmi I have a remedy for this malady.
   I can help.

Kayode I –

Matanmi Just trust me.

Kayode I dunno you.

Matanmi You can trust me.

Kayode You walk in here, sayin –

Matanmi Be calm, Kayode –

Kayode I –

*Itan pats him on the back.
He takes a deep breath.*

Matanmi I can help.

Kayode Are you cursed?

Matanmi No, but –

Kayode Exactly.
Matanmi I was.

Kayode You were –
Matanmi But it was reversed.

Kikiope How?
Kayode How?

Matanmi Prayer.

Kayode I pray.
  We pray.

Matanmi Maybe, but –
Kayode So if it's as simple as that –

Matanmi It isn't.

Kayode It ain't juss prayer then?

Matanmi It's prayer, but –

Kayode I don't –

Matanmi Kayode, be calm.
Kikiope Kayode, let's lissen.

Kayode I am.
  I'm juss
  confused,
  thass all.

> *Itan hands him a cup of tea,*
> *massages his shoulders.*

Matanmi I understand, but I wouldn't bring you bad news
with no solution.
  You can trust me.

Kayode I . . .

–

–

Alright.

Matanmi You were cursed, but it can be rendered null and void.

Kayode Mmm.

Matanmi You don't believe.

Kayode I do, but –

Matanmi We wrestle not against –

Kayode Ephesians 6:12.
I know the Word, Pastor.

Matanmi (*lightly*) Then why do you look at me like I'm an idiot?

Kayode I'm not.
I'm juss . . .
Issa surprise.

Matanmi Don't worry, Kayode.
The Lord can reverse it.
We'll sing.
We'll pray.
We'll battle.

Kayode And then?

Matanmi Let's focus on that for now.

Kayode How long's it meant to take?

Matanmi 'With the Lord a day is like a thousand years, and a thousand years are like a day.'

–

Kikiope Pastor, can we sleep on this?

Matanmi Of course.
　　You have my number
　　so call me when you're ready,
　　when revelation envelops your eyes.
　　I pray it'll surprise and come soon.

Kikiope Thank you, Pastor, I'll walk out with –

Kayode D'you know why?

Matanmi Why what?
Kikiope Kayode.

Kayode Why it happened.

Matanmi The curse?

Kayode Yeah.
　　You said . . .
　　I don't get why . . .
　　Why would a woman steal me
　　as a baby an'
　　curse me to –

Matanmi I don't know.

Kayode But you said –

Matanmi I only saw what the Lord presented.

Kayode But can you –

Matanmi I don't speculate, Kayode.
　　But we could uncover the answers.
　　Through our prayer,
　　the Lord may allow us to discover that.

Kayode I see.

–

Matanmi Call me, son.

Kayode Yes, Pastor.

Matanmi Goodbye, Kikiope. God bless.

Kikiope Thank you, sir.
  Let me –

Matanmi It's fine. I know the way.

> *Matanmi exits.*
> *We hear the door shut and*
> *Kikiope laughs.*

Kayode Why you lau—

Kikiope He's crazy.

Kayode You think –

Kikiope How dare he?

Kayode What'd you –
Kikiope Comin round –

Kayode He –
Kikiope An' tellin you you're cursed?
  Ain't right.

Kayode I –

Kikiope You lived in Nigeria for one month.
  Who curses a newborn baby?

Kayode When you put it like that –

Kikiope It's mad.

> *They laugh.*
> *Itan too,*
> *then she leaves.*

How'd you meet him?

Kayode Church.

Kikiope Ours?

20

Kayode Yeah.

Kikiope When?

Kayode I went to the toilet –

Kikiope How apt.
Kayode An' he stopped me juss outside.
    Seemed genuine.
    Said he had his own church,
    but was visitin that day
    knowin I'd be there.

Kikiope I should complain.

Kayode Why?

Kikiope Ain't right, is it?
    Charismatics wormin their way into lives.
    Preyin on the vulnerable.

Kayode I ain't vulnerable.

Kikiope I dint mean you.
Kayode I get down sometimes, but we all do.
    Yesterday, you were –

Kikiope I dint mean you.

Kayode Right.

Kikiope But tellin you he can overthrow a curse
    an' secure you employment.
    Issa scam.
    Like SPAC,
    these men spoutin crap
    manipulatin faith
    twistin it
    reshapin it
    for their benefit?
    It's disgustin.
    Pushes people away.

Steals their truth.
An' y'know they're gonna go to hell for –

Kayode Keeks, chill.
Ain't that deep.

Kikiope It ain't right.

Kayode Who would you even complain to?

Kikiope Church.

Kayode An' what'll they do?
Can't stop people comin in.

Kikiope I know, I juss . . .
He's speakin like
your employment's in
HIS hands.
As if you've been waitin
for him
this whole time.

Kayode Right.

–

Kikiope Speakin of work, I . . .
I've got sum news.

–

Kayode What, you pregnant?

Kikiope God, no.

Kayode Ah, thass a shame,
I've already nailed the stay-at-home-dad thing.

She forces a chuckle.
A small one.

Whass wrong?

Kikiope Nothin, I . . . It's good.

22

Kayode Good.
Kikiope I, er, I got offered a promotion today.

Kayode Keeks, thass amazin.

Kikiope Head of Digital.

Kayode Look at you.

Kikiope It's nothin.
Kayode Well done, Keeks.

Kikiope I ain't accepted it yet.

Kayode Why not?

Kikiope Had to talk to you first.

Kayode I wouldn't tell you not to.

Kikiope I know, but still.
　You're my husband, ain't you?

Kayode Hope you're gettin a raise too.

Kikiope We're talkin numbers.

Kayode Good.
Kikiope I asked for fifty K.

Kayode Fifty?

Kikiope Yeah.

Kayode Five-zero?

Kikiope Yup.

Itan enters,
whistling,
hoovering.

Kayode Jeez, Keeks, thass brill—

Kayode's head spins
towards Itan.

Itan waves, childlike.

Kikiope They'll prob'ly offer forty-five
but issa small company so thass still –

Kayode Oh, God.

–

Kikiope What?

–

Kayode?

–

Kayode?

TWO

A multitude of offices
over several years.

Kayode interviews,
with Itan at his side.

1 (*voice-over*) Why do you want this job?

Kayode I've admired this charity for years. Your values align with mine and I wanna help –

2 (*voice-over*) What are your greatest professional achievements?

Kayode At uni, I held an event at a young offenders institute, and through that we ended up creating a programme –

3 (*voice-over*) Tell me about a challenge or conflict you've faced at work and how you dealt with it.

Kayode Several days before we were meant to start our programme, we received a call from the prison wanting to cancel because –

4 (*voice-over*) What type of work environment do you consider ideal?

Kayode I love a calm, fun and inspiring workplace. I value teamwork, while –

5 (*voice-over*) Where do you see yourself in five years?

Kayode I'd love to move to the country with my wife and start a charity, one that isn't too London-centric, in order to –

5 (*voice-over*) Where do you see yourself in five years?

Kayode Living in the country with my wife, running a –

5 (*voice-over*) Where do you see yourself in five years?
Itan *uff un yi xemen yi missa eyle bret*

> *Kayode flinches.*

Kayode Sorry, could you repeat the question?

6 (*voice-over*) If you could invite three people to dinner – dead or alive – who would they be? And why?

Kayode Honestly? I'd invite my wife. My mum and dad too, though I never knew –

7 (*voice-over*) How do you deal with stressful situations?

Kayode Communication's key, so I always ensure –

8 (*voice-over*) Tell us something that isn't on your CV?

Kayode I love –

4 (*voice-over*) What type of work environment do you consider ideal?
Itan *utu grit pwe verne whuq un yi kivann zree*

> *Kayode whips his head around,*
> *then back forward.*

Kayode Sorry, could you repeat –

7 (*voice-over*) How do you deal with stressful situations?

Kayode I –
1 (*voice-over*) Why do you want this job?

Kayode This compa—
9 (*voice-over*) What is your biggest weakness?

Kayode My biggest –
3 (*voice-over*) Tell me about a challenge or conflict you've faced at work –

Kayode At uni I held a –

2 (*voice-over*) What are your greatest professional achieve—

> *Questions continue*
> *overlapping as*
> *Kayode attempts to answer.*

> *Then he stalls,*
> *overwhelmed.*

> *Itan embraces him.*

Itan Shhh.

> *She whistles.*
> *The voices simmer*
> *until there's silence.*

–

8 (*voice-over*) Tell us something that isn't on your CV?

THREE

*Kikiope is preparing to leave.
She puts on her jacket,
picks up her keys,
packs the last items into her bag*

*as Itan helps Kayode change
out of his wet T-shirt
and put his shoes/jacket on.*

Kayode I was cursed.

Kikiope Kayode –

Kayode I can feel it.

Kikiope D'you have a nightmare or somethin?

Kayode Nothin.
I juss know
he was tellin the truth.
It's the reason for all this.

Kikiope How'd you know that?

He looks at Itan.

Kayode It's obvious now.

Kikiope I don't think –

Kayode Why else would my life be like this?

Kikiope You ain't –

Kayode Keeks, I know it sounds weird,
but I think it's why

28

it's been so hard.
Why I . . .

Kikiope He was a fraud.

Kayode I know you think so, but –

Kikiope I'm late, but I can text you Dr Davis's number?

Kayode Dr Davi—
Kikiope Speak to her.

Kayode I can speak to Pastor Mat—

Kikiope She gives good advice.

Kayode Lots of people can give advice.

Kikiope She's helped me.

Kayode She can't reverse the curse.

Kikiope I juss – Why's your jacket on?
Kayode She'll be wastin her time.

Kikiope Kayode, she –

Kayode I've gotta to see him.

Kikiope No, you –

Kayode It's been over seven years, Keeks.

Kikiope I know, but –

Kayode Can't even get a job in a shop.

Kikiope I know, but –
Kayode Or pickin rubbish off of the ground.

Kikiope Can we get into this later?

Kayode Alright.
Kikiope It's juss I'm gonna miss my –

Kayode It's fine, Keeks.

Kikiope We can call him tonight.

Kayode I can't sit here all day doin nothin, when –

Kikiope Kayode.

Kayode This is urgent.

Kikiope I wanna be there.

Kayode Call in sick then.

Kikiope I juss got offered a promotion.

Kayode I can't wait till tonight, Keeks.

Kikiope Please.
Kayode I can feel it in my bones.
  He's exactly what I've needed.
  He's gonna guide me
  like the star led the wise.

Kikiope Or maybe issa word
  conjured up by pound signs
  in his eyes.

Kayode He ain't gettin nothin.

Kikiope Yet.
  But if you get a job –

Kayode When.

Kikiope What?

Kayode When I get a job.

Kikiope Thass what I said.
  When you get a job an'
  he asks you to move to his church –
  you'd do it, right?

  –

Exactly.
    Then where's your tithe goin?
    His pockets.

Kayode Keeks,
    his word . . .
    Issa prophecy.
    Issa key
    to my success.

Kikiope Kayode –

Kayode You're annoyed.

Kikiope No, I'm late.

Kayode Fine.

> *He takes off his jacket and*
> *throws it to the ground.*
>
> *Itan shakes her head,*
> *picks and hangs it up,*
> *then goes to rest.*

Kikiope Thank you.
Kayode I'll see you later.
    I love you.

Kikiope Love you too.

> *Kikiope heads out,*
> *then stops.*

You not gonna take off your shoes?

Kayode You're gonna miss your train.

Kikiope This is crazy.

Kayode I ain't crazy.

Kikiope Dint say you were, I –

Kayode You think Pastor Matanmi –

Kikiope He's not a pastor.

Kayode You think he's a joke.

Kikiope No, it's juss –
Kayode Keeks.
　　This hex has festered,
　　its roots have been stuck
　　for almost three decades.
　　I've been oblivious
　　but now I know.
　　The Lord has made it known.
　　I can't ignore it now it's known.
　　Gotta battle.
　　Gotta fight.

Kayode turns to Itan.

It's always been there.
　　Lingering.

Kikiope I don't –

Kayode I thought it was Comfort, y'see?
　　When I was a child,
　　she'd help me
　　with little things.
　　We'd laugh, dance,
　　sing our songs.
　　But after Pastor spoke
　　I now see the strings bein played,
　　the masquerade.
　　How the curse manifested.

Kikiope Or you could be makin
　　one plus one equal three.

Kayode No.
　　He was talkin bout breakin chains.

Breakin cycles.
Breakin captivity.
Freedom from tyranny.
The enemy.
Thass what I need.
Thass the remedy.

Kikiope We go to church.

Kayode To do what?
Stand an' sing hymn 771.
Then sit,
then stand.

Kikiope We read the Word.

Kayode So do they.

Kikiope Kayode, I've gotta –

Kayode Then go. If you don't believe in –

Kikiope Who said I don't?

Kayode Then why ain't you lissenin?
Kikiope I know they're real.
I know curses exists.

Kayode Then accept it.
Juju's manifestin stagnancy,
policin me.
I want to enter life anew.
Renewed.
Without my destiny screwed
skewered
by the witches and wizards of Lagos.

–

–

Kikiope He'll warp your soul.

Kayode WHAT soul?

–

Kikiope Whass that supposed to mean?

–

–

Kayode.
    If you're feelin a way,
    I want you to tell me.

Kayode I'm fine.

–

Kikiope Y'know I love you, right?

Kayode I love you too.
    Thass why I've gotta –

Kikiope Then name it.
    Let's name it.

–

Kayode Pastor Matanmi's a warrior.

Kikiope Messin with all o' that ain't a joke, Kayode.

Kayode I know, but I've already made up my mind.
    Y'know why?
    Cos this is the happiest I've been in time.
    The most hopeful I've felt.

–

I see a light movin my way.

FOUR

Layo's flat.

*Kikiope sits as Layo picks stones
out of her bowl of beans.*

Layo Do you want anything to drink?
I have Malt, Shloer –

Kikiope No, thank you, Aunty, I'm –

Layo Ah, before I forget, I bought this new prayer book.
I thought you'd like it, so I got you a –
What's wrong?

–

Why're you shaking?
Is Kayode . . .

Kikiope He's not well.

Layo Is it cancer?

Kikiope No.
No.
I . . .

Layo Kikiope?

Kikiope He's d . . .
He's adrift again.

Layo I don't –

Kikiope Meltin like ice.

*Layo kisses her teeth,
continues picking.*

Layo Kikiope, I don't know what –

Kikiope Aunty –

Layo What is it, *jo*?

Kikiope I need your help speakin to Kayode.
He think he's been cursed.
This pastor cornered him
spoutin lies
tying him to this idea
that a woman –

Layo Pastor Matanmi isn't lying.

–

Kikiope How'd –

Layo He's helping us.

Kikiope You know bout this?

Layo Kikiope, listen.
What Kayode's been going through . . .
It isn't normal.

Kikiope I know, Aunty, I –
Layo And I had my share of enemies in Nigeria.

Kikiope He only lived there for a month.

Layo And?
Nigerians do juju like it's nothing.
Going to the Babalawo
is an everyday occurrence, Kikiope.

Kikiope It's not witchcraft.

Layo It is.
The Lord showed me and I went to Pastor Matanmi.

Kikiope You went to him?

Layo He's my new pastor.
I cried in his office.
Told him about my struggles.
Told him about my pains.
Told him about my Kayode.
And as we prayed, he saw.
He had a similar vision
before I even told him
about the curse itself.

Kikiope And you trust him?

Layo Why else would I introduce them?

Kikiope You dint. They met –

Layo I asked him to go to your church, Kikiope.
Kayode wouldn't listen
to the words that cascade from my lips.
He would think I was mad.
Wonder why I've buried the knowledge
of my visions;
knowledge of these spirits
that follow us;
these curses
that destroy us.
I've destroyed all things ancestral
within me.
I thought it would protect Kayode
but he needs to do it himself.

Kikiope Aunty –

Layo Juju is real, Kikiope.

Kikiope I know.

Layo Spirits battle.

Kikiope I know, but I know Kayode.

Layo And I don't?
 Shebi, I gave birth to him?

Kikiope Of course, Aunty –

Layo Exactly.
Kikiope But I don't want him goin through with sum ceremony.

Layo It's just seventy-two hours of fasting, Kikiope.

Kikiope Just?

Layo I've done it before.

Kikiope He ain't strong enough for that.

Layo Kikiope,
 I know your British
 mind
 may struggle to understand –

Kikiope No, I get it –

Layo So why not let us work to fight it?
Kikiope An' it's got nothin to do with bein British –

Layo No? You've never gone home.

Kikiope That doesn't –
Layo You've never set foot there,
 so how can you understand?

Kikiope It ain't bout what I've done
 nor where I've gone, Aunty –

Layo *Shebi*, I taught you to make pounded yam?

Kikiope I –
Layo Eba. Egusi. Asaro.
 Me, not your mother.

Kikiope This has nothin to do with –

38

Layo You don't have the knowledge,
my dear,
and no amount of reading
will make it your home.

FIVE

Kayode and Kikiope's sitting room.
Matanmi and Kayode are together.

Itan too, observing Matanmi suspiciously.

Matanmi Do you feel ready?

Kayode nods.

Good.

–

I like you, Kayode.
    You're going to change the world.
    I can feel it.

Kayode (*jokingly*) Gotta get rid o' this curse first.

Matanmi Of course.

–

Will Kikiope be bringing the oil?

Kayode No, erm, er . . .
    My mum's in the area.
    She's bringin it.

Matanmi Oh. Well, it would be nice to have Kikiope join us.

Kayode She won't.
    She thinks I'm . . .
    Keeps tellin me to see her counsellor.

Matanmi Isaiah 9:6 tells us He –
Kayode Like she thinks I'm weak.

Matanmi You can't be weak and battle with spirits.

Kayode I know.

Matanmi Be careful about those who don't believe you.

Kayode I will.
Matanmi You need discernment
Or this employment you're after . . .
It will be a patch of soil that remains dry
even in the midst of a rainstorm.

–

–

I used to be married myself.

Kayode You?
Matanmi She was the sun and I the beach.
Picture perfect.
We would swim in the seas of
Antibes, Amalfi, Athens.
Eat at the Ritz, Regis, Rosewood.
But in the dark, we were living in sin.
Drugs, drink, everything.
Then I saw Him.
I saw the light that shone on my life.
There was something better written in the book
that I'd abandoned, 'cause I was afraid to look,
but He forced me to glance.
Not just glance, but see.
And in that book I saw me and our church
built by man's hands.
Built by following His demands.
So I knew I had to heed.

Only, my wife didn't believe.

We fought and, often, the web caught me
several times.

So I prayed.
I prayed for God to move the boulder
The boulder threatening that I shan't get older
but stumble and fall
and put God's calling for me in the bin.
'Cause I wanted to be the one that did it.
'Cause He can get anyone to do it.
And He can give anyone that job
that should be yours.

Kayode I know.
Matanmi He wants you, but there are many.
And there are many,
like your wife, who can stand
in the way –
steal
your destiny.
Such was my wife.
So I prayed.

I shatter barriers, blockages,
barricades, and boulders.

The following month, my wife died.
A bad combination of drugs and drink.

Did I cry? Yes.
I loved her.
But, in spite of it, I had to dance.
Through pain, I was given a chance
to flourish.
To finally water my seed.
Do what I needed to do.
And now it's my job,
To make sure others do the same.

–

Kayode Kikiope isn't standin in my way.

Matanmi It sounds like –
Kayode She's juss tired.

Matanmi Son, trust me, I get it.
    When the Lord takes –
    especially that which one loves
    more than anything in the world–
    it hurts.
    Look at Job.
    But the Lord restores, son.
    Gives you those you can lean on.

> *Matanmi puts his hand*
> *on Kayode's shoulder.*

> *The door opens,*
> *Layo enters.*

Layo Sorry, I'm late.

Kayode It's fine, Mum. Let me introduce you to –

Layo Pastor Matanmi.

Matanmi Sister Layo.

Kayode How d'you know each other?

Layo He's my new pastor.

Kayode You're –
Matanmi Kayode said his mother was bringing the oil,
but I –

Layo Yes.
    (*Handing over the oil.*) Here.

Matanmi Thank you, sister.

Kayode Thanks, Mum.
    I'll see you later.

Layo I'd like to stay.

Kayode You don't need –
Layo I want to join in prayer.

Kayode Mum –

Layo If you're cursed –
Kayode We'll be fine.

Matanmi Kayode, let her join.
There is no prayer more powerful
than that of a desperate mother.

–

–

Shall we begin?

Layo Yes.

Matanmi takes the oil.

Matanmi O, Lord, may your anointing be upon this oil.
Guide and protect us as we go into battle.
May your angels envelop us against all spirits
that don't want your will to come to pass,
in the mighty name of Jesus.
Amen.

Kayode Amen.
Layo Amen.

Matanmi opens the oil,
pours some onto his palm.

Uses his finger to draw a cross
on the foreheads of Kayode
Layo and himself.

Matanmi In the name of Jesus
I bind every strongman
delegated to hinder Kayode's progress.

Kayode I bind every strongman
  delegated to hinder my progress.
Layo I bind every strongman
  delegated to hinder Kayode's progress.

Matanmi I bind you.

Kayode I bind you. I bind you. I bind you.
  I bind you. I bind you. I bind you –
Matanmi I bind you. I bind you. I bind you.
  I bind you. I bind you. I bind you . . .
Layo I bind you. I bind you. I bind you.
  I bind you. I bind you. I bind you . . .

Matanmi Amen.

Kayode Amen.
Layo Amen.

Matanmi In the name of Jesus,
  I purge Kayode of all evil planted within.
  Purge him. Purge him.

Layo Purge him. Purge him. Purge him.
  Purge him. Purge Kayode Aarinola
  Inioluwa Oluwafikayomi Falola.
  Purge him. Purge him, I beg. Purge –
Matanmi Purge him. Purge him. Purge him.
  Purge him. Purge him. Purge him.
  Purge him. Purge him. Purge him.
  Purge him. Purge him. Purge him –
Kayode Purge me. Purge me. Purge me.
  Purge me. Purge me. Purge me.
  Purge me. Purge me. Purge me.
  Purge me. Purge me. Purge me.

Matanmi Amen.

Layo Amen.
Kayode Amen.

Matanmi O, Lord, send your axe of fire
  upon all ungodly spirits cleaving to Kayode
  and destroy them.

Itan stands,
approaches them.

Itan *utu seeg yi unkana*
Layo O, Lord, send your axe of fire
  upon all ungodly spirits cleaving to Kayode
  and destroy them.
Kayode O, Lord, send your axe of fire
  upon all ungodly spirits cleavin to me
  and destroy them.

Itan screams.

Itan *UTU SEEG YI UNKANA*

Matanmi Destroy them. Destroy them. Destroy them.
Layo Destroy them. Destroy them. Destroy them.
Kayode Destroy em. Destroy em. Destroy em. Destroy em.
Itan Kayode, *heynen, heynen reinn.* Kayode.

Itan screams again.

Matanmi Destroy them. Destroy them. Destroy them.
Layo Destroy them. Destroy them. Destroy them.
Kayode Destroy em. Destroy em. Destroy em. Destroy em.
Itan *y kivantar yi seegt rikana tieen pwe rei mernp*

Itan grunts
stumbles, bleeds.

Matanmi Destroy them. Destroy them. Destroy them . . .
Layo Destroy them. Destroy them. Destroy them . . .
Kayode Destroy em. Destroy em. Destroy em . . .
Itan *un yi kivann reinn vernet . . . heen.*
  yex quih udoj erfe
  erfe/erfe/erfe/erfe/erfe

Itan falls,
freezes time.

Itan KAYODE.

Kayode *heen*

Itan I am not the curse.

Kayode *heen*

Itan I'm protesting in this wild tongue,
this tongue that I despise.
Does that not prove that fact?

Kayode *qleed*

Itan I've always been here.
I'm family.
History.

Kayode I don't care.
I'm done.
I wanna be cleansed.
Free of all bondage.

Itan You don't have to get rid of me.

Kayode *QLEED*

Itan *utu seeg yi unkana*
hinz frimn y
yerhy udoj moos bas ushung

Kayode DIE.

Itan Okay.
yi udoj xemen
y puntu fylk giigra

Kayode reaches out
to Matanmi.
He touches him,
unfreezing things.

47

Kayode ARGH.
Matanmi ARGH.

–

What was that?

Kayode She's there.

Matanmi Who?
Layo Let's continue. We can't waste one minute.
Itan *bas qlenza uxeb menna dallt ra y*

Layo Pastor.

Matanmi Sorry. I, er . . .

Layo O, Lord, let all that is in Kayode's foundation which is not of you, disappear.

Kayode O, Lord, let all that is in my foundation which is not of you, disappear.
Matanmi (*delayed, still spooked*) O, Lord, let all that is in Kayode's foundation which is not of you, disappear.

> *Itan continues to struggle*
> *weaken*
> *pant.*

Kayode Disappear. Disappear. Disappear.
   Disappear. Disappear. Disappear.
   Disappear. Disappear. Disappear.
   Disappear. Disappear. Disappear.
   Disappear. Disappear. Disappear.
Layo Disappear. Disappear. Disappear.
   Disappear. Disappear. Disappear.
   Disappear. Disappear. Disappear.
   Disappear. Disappear. Disappear.
   Disappear. Disappear. Disappear.
Matanmi Disappear. Disappear. Disappear.
   Disappear. Disappear. Disappear.
   Disappear. Disappear. Disappear.

Disappear. Disappear. Disappear.
Disappear. Disappear. Disappear.
Itan *heynen lemento yi mein*
yi udoj mein, Kayode
y udoj vind menna yent wotlyneh
y'oole mklena
y – ARGHHHHHH.

Itan crawls away,
still bleeding.

Itan *y udoj dall toogoo,* Kayode – *giigraxuhn*
Kayode Disappear. Disappear. Disap—
Matanmi Disappear. Disappear. Disappear . . .
Layo Disappear. Disappear. Disappear . . .

She leaves
and Kayode feels this.

He stops.
Opens his eyes.
Looks around.
Grins.

SIX

Kayode praises,
beaming the entire time
singing his own rhyme

despite occasionally stopping
to breathe,
clutching his stomach.

Kayode *She's gone from my life.*
I thank you, Lord.
She's gone from my life.
I thank you, Lord.

Kikiope enters, watches.

She's gone from my life.
I thank you, Lord.

Kikiope Who's she?

–

Kayode Don't worry.

He continues to sing,
stumbles slightly
several times.

She's gone from my life.
I thank you, Lord.

Kikiope Kayode,
you should eat somethin.

Kayode Only twenty-six hours left.

Kikiope Kayode –

Kayode I'm fine.
   It'll be gone
   for good
   after this.

Kikiope Okay.

Kayode *She's gone from my life.*
   I thank – Dance with me, Keeks.

Kikiope I, er, okay.

Kayode *She's gone from my life.*
   I thank you, Lord.

Kikiope *She's gone from my life, I –*
Kayode *She's gone from my life –*
   You're doin it wrong.

Kikiope Oh.
   Sorry.

Kayode *She's gone from my life.*

Kikiope *I thank you, Lord.*
Kayode *I thank you –*
   Y'know what?
   Don't worry.
   You don't have to –
   I can –

                              Kikiope steps aside.

She's gone from my –

                              Kayode falls.

I'm fine.

Kikiope D'you want sum water?

Kayode I can't have –

51

Kikiope Oh
    yeah
    sorry

Kayode Don't worry.
    I'm juss gonna sit for a bit.

Kikiope Cool.

> *He gets up immediately*
> *and continues.*

Kayode *She's gone from my –*

> *He falls again.*

Kayode Ugh.
Kikiope Kayode –

Kayode I'm fine. I'm fine.

Kikiope You ain—
Kayode *I'm free now.*

> *He rises again.*
> *Kikiope puts her head*
> *in her hands, distressed.*

Kayode *Don't need anyone but you, Lord.*
Kikiope Kayode, please.

Kayode *She's gone and it's just us.*

SEVEN

Matanmi's church.
Matanmi and Kikiope are
opposite one another.

Over this, Kayode is still
dancing and singing
and stumbling.

Kikiope He's not well.

Matanmi The fasting can be difficult.

Kikiope He's runnin a fever, he –

Matanmi He's being cleansed.

Kikiope Can you speak to him?
He'll only listen to you.

Matanmi There's no need for me to interject.
This is part of the process.

Kikiope What if I told you he . . .
I don't think it's that simple.
I think he's de . . .
He was dejected, thass all it was
but now –

Matanmi He'll be fine.

Kikiope I think he's gettin worse.

Matanmi You're scared.

Kikiope Yeah, I am.
Matanmi But this isn't the best way forward.

Kikiope Then what is?
  I let you continue
  cos what other options were there?
  Job centre?
  Tried that, but they ain't helpful.
  They basically blame you.
  So I let you do the ceremony
  but I ain't sure it's worked.
  An' now he's goin seventy-two hours
  with no food or water.
  I know thass how you do things, but
  surely there are exceptions, if it's impactin health.

Matanmi This isn't your true worry, Kikiope.

Kikiope It is.

Matanmi Speak to me.
  I want to be here for you too.
  Guide you too.

Kikiope Guide me?

Matanmi Yes.
Kikiope How?
  You manipulate the Word and you want –

Matanmi No, I don't, Kikiope.

Kikiope D'you really think warfare's what Kayode needs
right –

Matanmi This isn't about Kayode.

Kikiope It is, he's –

Matanmi No, Kikiope. Be true to yourself.

Kikiope I don't need to be accountable to you.

Matanmi You're trying to control
  change
  the situation,

but the only thing you have agency over
is yourself.

Kikiope I know that.

Matanmi Then tell me how you're feeling.

Kikiope Ain't it clear? I'm tired, Pastor.
Matanmi If you don't vocalise it –

–

–

Kikiope It's been seven years.
I can't watch him get his hopes
up
only for em to fall,
crash
down
like a tsunami.
It'll destroy everythin.

–

Matanmi Pray with me, Kikiope.

Kikiope I –
Matanmi You desire the guidance of the Lord.
You desire to hear his voice.

Kikiope I hear his voice already.
I desire to move forward.

Matanmi Isn't that what we all want?

Kikiope I want him –
us –
to name it
for once.

Matanmi And I want him to be
free.

55

Kikiope There's no such thing
  as freedom
  here.
  The curse ain't a curse, but
  this country.
  Us here.
  Cost of living
  unemployment rates
  mental illness rates,
  higher than they've been in
  decades.

Matanmi A woman stole him
  in the middle of the night
  from his mother's room, Kikiope.
  Took him away,
  like he was nothing.

Kikiope You said.

Matanmi She put a curse upon him.
  Put a hex upon him.
  Deemed him to be a failure.
  Commanded that he savour pain.
  That he would sow no works,
  no perks.

Kikiope You can't be so sure.

Matanmi You're the only one who isn't.

Kikiope I ain't sayin the vision ain't true,
  but you can't say you know exactly
  how to fix this.

Matanmi I didn't say I did, but I felt it
  while we were praying.
  Kayode touched me
  and I felt it.

Kikiope Felt what?

Matanmi There's something . . .

His lip quivers.

There's a powerful spirit within Kayode, Kikiope.
   It needs to be broken
   or it might break through and
   leave him
   in pieces.

–

Kikiope An' if this fast doesn't work?

Matanmi It will.
   God wouldn't let him drown.
   I promise.

EIGHT

A couple of offices
over several days.

Kayode interviews.

1 (*voice-over*) Hello, Kayode, it's lovely to meet you.

Kayode Thanks for having me.

1 (*voice-over*) Tell us a bit about why you think you're the right person for this job?

Kayode Of course. Firstly, you're a charity that I –

> *Offstage, Itan screams,*
> *wiping Kayode's smile*
> *straight off his face.*

> *She enters*
> *wearing an extravagant*
> *wedding dress*
> *with a twenty-seven-foot train.*

Itan (*to Kayode*) *tili? tili?*
muku rett utu yi tantim padd, Kayode?
muku rett utu yi tantim iang yus?

(*To audience.*) **It isn't what he wants.**
You heard him say I was Comfort, right?
I know you heard it.

Kayode You're a charity I greatly admire.

> *Itan flinches,*
> *as Kayode continues*
> *unfazed by her disruption.*

58

But for me it's about those young men.
    I know I can reach them and I'll be someone
    who they can identify with.

2 (*voice-over*) What are your greatest professional
achievements?

Kayode The moment I'm proudest of was a little while
back actually.

> *Itan scoops water into her hands,*
> *throws it around, as if casting a spell.*

I organised a prison event for young Black men,
    to help give them a sense of the possibil . . .

> *He looks at Itan.*
> *Takes a deep breath.*

Itan I'm love.
    We love each other.
    un yerhy heent

Kayode Possibilities the future . . .
    Possibilities the –

> *He puts his head in his hands.*
> *Whispers quietly to himself.*

Itan The universe made us as one
    knowing perfectly what we needed,
    something no prayer, medicine
    or performative expression of
    emotions can erase.

1 (*voice-over*) Why do you want this job?

Itan I love him.
    He loves me.

y crern yi
    y akavi yi

I need him, I do.
> What would I do if he wasn't here?
> I'd die.
> And it's only with me he can
> swallow this ugly world.

> *la uume y niemm*, Kayode.

2 (*voice-over*) Where do you see yourself in five years?

Itan *agoun y crien*
> *un heent vind y mein yii shimkana*
> *porzat ra lenke yee likkta*
> *reinn muku heent juplex*
> *menna muku crern*

1 (*voice-over*) Why do you want –

Itan *tili? tili?*

> > *Successfully interrupting,*
> > *Itan grins.*

TILI? TILI?
> *TOPI PUNTUQ YI?*
> *YERHY SEEG ASHGEN*

NINE

Layo's flat.
Layo, Kayode and Matanmi stand.

Kayode It's still here.
The curse still flows through my veins
like blood.

Matanmi Son, you must believe.

Kayode This ain't bout belief.
Ain't seen it yet, but
I can feel it.

Layo Feel what?

Kayode I dunno.
Thass why I came here.
For answers.

Matanmi Kayode, don't worry, it'll be fine.

Kayode FINE?

Layo Calm down, Kayode.
We don't choose God's timeline.

Matanmi No, but we can pray.

Kayode No.
No.

Matanmi Kayode, listen to me.
Layo Kayode, listen –
Kayode I'm done.

Matanmi Don't be foolish.

Kayode I don't believe anythin you say any more.

61

Matanmi I'm God's servant.
I wouldn't lie to you.

Kayode You're juss a man.
Men lie.

Matanmi I can help you, son.

Kayode Don't call me that.

Layo Kayode.

Kayode NO.
I'm done.
With both of you.
You're tryna drown me,
while pretendin you're lifeboats.
Who said I was cursed?
Him.
He did.
Who benefits from my presence?
Him.
He does.

Matanmi I just wanted to help.

Kayode So when I get my first pay cheque
you can claim glory
Take my money.

Layo Kayode, behave.
Matanmi No, Kayode, you could accuse me
of not using wisdom but you –

Kayode It was all bout your ego.

Matanmi I care about you, Kayode.
I've shared my pain with you.

Kayode You mean your dance over your dead wife?

Layo Kayode, stop.
Matanmi Don't twist my words, Kayode.

Kayode I'm not.
Matanmi I care about you,
    want you to thrive
    and you think I'm doing this for money?
    Do you think that lowly of me?

Layo Kayode.
Kayode I don't KNOW you.

Layo Let's calm down.

Matanmi I've been trying to help.
    Do I have to get on my knees to prove that?

Kayode Yes, Pastor, get on your –

                          Layo slaps Kayode.

Matanmi (*taking her aside*) Sister.

Layo Pastor, can you give us a moment?

Matanmi I don't think –
Layo I need to speak with my son.

Matanmi You came to me, because you were scared for him.

Layo I know, but if we push him too hard, he might . . .

Matanmi He won't.

Layo We don't know that.

Matanmi You must have faith.

Layo I shouldn't have come to you.
    Just because God told us something,
    it didn't mean we were meant to tell Kayode.

Matanmi Of course we were.

Layo I didn't ask God if this is what we were meant to do.

Matanmi But I did.

Layo I don't know if I believe that.

Matanmi What good are our gifts if we don't use them
to edify one another?

Layo Sir, with all due respect,
I would like to be alone
with my son.

Matanmi scoffs.

Matanmi To each their own, sister Layo.
May God bless you both.

Matanmi exits.

Kayode How did he know where I went to church?

–

Layo I knew you wouldn't listen to me, you –

Kayode I dint delve into it
cos I juss wanted the curse gone, undone,
but you were deceivin me this whole time.

Layo It wasn't deception.

Kayode You lied.

Layo The Lord's people keep secrets, Kayode.
Esther kept –

Kayode You're a hypocrite.

Layo We had the same vision, Kayode.
Pastor Matanmi and I saw –
separately, we saw –
a woman steal you in the middle of the night.
From my room.

Kayode I've heard all of this.

Layo I saw this woman
cook up stew and
command it to savour pain.
Upon you, my baby, but only

64

from grown age.
Once school's out of the way;
after you do so well.
Get As.
A degree.
Another degree.
Do everything you're supposed to.
She commanded the stew
to sow no work.
No perks.
A beautiful wife.
But strife.
No climbs.
And then I saw her feed it to you.
Let you swallow each spoon.
Savour the doom . . .
Do you think it's easy to tell my son that?
Do you think I can sleep at night after seeing that?
I had to seek counsel, Kayode.

Kayode If I've got an abundance of spirits
    principalities
    demons
    dwellin
    within me,
    thass your fault.

Layo It is not my fault.

Kayode Why should I believe you?

Layo I'm your mum.

–

Kayode Who was she?

Layo Who?

Kayode The woman who cursed me.

Layo I . . . I don't know.

Kayode You've gotta.

Layo I don't.

Kayode So, you're tellin me –

Layo Kayode, it doesn't matter what happened, it –

Kayode You're unbelievable.

Layo Kayode.
Kayode I don't trust you.
   You just know that Keeks
   doesn't want children
   with a man who had so much
   promise
   an' now has no future –

Layo Kayode, *jo*.
   This isn't about you earning millions
   or grandchildren galore.
   God knows I don't care about that.
   This is about
   freedom
   from the sins of our forefathers.
   You are under bondage.
   I just want you
   to be free.

Kayode Mum, stop.
   STOP.
   juss live your life, okay?
   an' I'll live mine.
   Strife or no strife.
   Alright?

TEN

Kayode and Kikiope's flat.

Kayode I know you're there.

*Itan enters, carrying a suit
that matches her dress.*

She hangs it up.

Itan Hello, Kayode.

Kayode *tili jalaha*

Itan *heen*

Kayode Lord, send her away.

Itan Shhh.

She hugs Kayode.

Kayode I fasted for three days straight and –

Itan Save your breath.

Kayode I hate you.

Itan That's what got us here.
You tried to kill me,
when I was innocently living.

Kayode Lord, I –

Itan Don't bother.
We're bound,
Adam.
Isn't it glorious?
Majestic?

–

67

Us.

–

Kayode.
    As I've said,
    you know how I hate
    this wild tongue,
    but I'm using it because I
    want you to see me as family as I
    apologise.
    I want you to release me.
    Let me flow down the stream.
    With serenity.

She laughs.

I'm just kidding.
    Serenity can be a drag.
    I tried it before,
    but you wanted war.

Kayode *riksaw y*

Itan I told you, I can't.
    We're bound.
    I'm History, babe –
    more powerful than juju –
    determined to stay,
    and not just stay this time.
    Not just linger.
    I want to be accepted.
    I want you to say 'I do'.
    I've waited too long.

–

Kayode *qleed*

Itan If I die, so will you.

Kayode *y'oole heina*

Itan I know.
Kayode *masck y inkitar mklen numar ra fylk*

Itan Do we really have to go there?
Is not easier to accept me?

Kayode *y inkitar mklen numar ra fylk*

Itan Fine,
but you hurt me badly
last time
so I've brought some moral support.

> *Itan clicks her finger.*

> *The witches and wizards*
> *of Lagos chant.*
> *Loudly.*

Kayode O, Lord, I destroy anything
cursing my life, in the mighty
name of Jesus.
I destroy it. I destroy it. I destroy it.
I destroy it. I –

Itan I'm not cursing you, Kayode.
How many times do I have to say it?
I'm History.
Yes, that means I *could* curse you –
hence why I've brought
the witches and wizards of Lagos
to accompany me here –
but I choose not to
as long as you hold me close.
Make me yours.

Kayode You're insane.

Itan Aren't we all?

–

Kayode I reverse every ruling
   given to any power
   to supervise my life.

Itan starts to bleed.

Itan Kayode.
Kayode O, Lord, send your axe of fire
   upon all ungodly spirits cleaving to me
   and destroy them.

Itan bleeds, groans.
Chants grow louder.

See.

Itan Stop.
Kayode I know what I'm doin.

Itan I've never lied to you, Kayode.

Kayode O, Lord, let all that is in my foundation
   which is not of you, disappear.

Itan ARGH.
   Kayode –

Kayode You're not meant to be here.

Itan That's a lie they've let you believe, but I'm a part –

Kayode Every power calling my name
   fall down and die,
   by the power in the blood of Jesus.

Itan (*to the witches and wizards*) DO BETTER.

Chants are at their loudest.

Kayode die
   die
   die
   die
   die

die
die

LOUDER THAN THE LOUDEST
but still Itan is in pain.

Die
Die
Die
Die
Die
Die
Die

DIe.
DIe.
DIe

DIe. DIe.
DIe. DIe.

DIE. DIE. DIE. DIE. DIE. DIE. DIE.
DIEDIEDIEDIEDIEDIEDIE –

Kayode's body moves
like a leaf
in the midst of a tsunami.

Then he collapses.
Silence.

Itan takes a tourniquet
from her hair;
she ties it around herself
reducing the bleeding.

She goes towards Kayode,
picks his head up.
Kisses his forehead.

His eyes open.

Itan Wake up.

Kayode Get off me.

Itan Kayode, I just saved you.

Kayode LEAVE ME.

Itan I GET DRESSED UP
FOR YOU, KAYODE,
AND THIS IS HOW YOU REPAY ME?

Kayode BE QUIET
Itan I DRESS UP FOR OUR REUNION

Kayode I BEG YOU
Itan SAVE YOU FROM
THE WITCHES AND WIZARDS –

Kayode I'M TIRED
Itan OF LAGOS
AND THIS IS HOW YOU –

She laughs.

Ohmygosh, I'm hilarious.

Kayode I'm gonna kill you.

Itan I saved you.

Kayode You called em.

Itan And I have the power to destroy them.
You can have all the good things,
a job, a wife
as long as you don't forget me.

Kayode I can't be tied to you.
Not in this world.

Itan But the curse has gone.

–

God told me.

–

Kayode Good.
  Now you can go with it.

Itan That would be a mistake.

Kayode I mean it.

Itan Okay.

> *She clicks her finger.*
> *The witches and wizards*
> *of Lagos begin to chant*
> *again, loudly.*
>
> *Kayode's body moves*
> *like a leaf*
> *in the midst of a tsunami*
> *as Itan laughs.*
>
> *He fights this feeling,*
> *charges towards her.*
>
> *The chanting continues*
> *as Kayode and Itan*
> *wrestle*
> *wrangle*
> *battle.*
>
> *He grabs her head*
> *pushes it into the water.*
> *She thrashes . . .*
>
> *grabs hold of him.*
> *He shakes her off.*
> *She thrashes . . .*
> *till still.*
>
> *Kayode catches his breath.*

ELEVEN

Kayode and Kikiope's sitting room.

Kikiope How was swimmin?

Kayode woke up late

Kikiope Kayode –

Kayode i'll go next week

Kikiope Alright.
D'you go on your walk?

Kayode yup
barking road an' back

Kikiope How'd it feel?

Kayode gd

Kikiope Good.
An' how was the interview?

Kayode i, er . . .
dint go

Kikiope Why not?

Kayode Yesterday's one drained me.

Kikiope Kayode, you shou—
Kayode I juss – Please don't.

–

–

Kikiope You want somethin to eat?

Kayode I'm fine, thanks.

–

Kikiope What's wrong?

Kayode The ceremony dint work.

Kikiope It's been a week an' you had two interviews.

Kayode I know, but –

Kikiope You ain't even got to that stage in years.

Kayode I don't wanna repeat it all again.
I can't do that any more, Keeks.

Kikiope It's worked, Kayode.

Kayode Has it?
Kikiope When you get a job, that'll juss confirm it.

Kayode What if I wasn't cursed?

Kikiope Kayo –

Kayode You said it.
What if it ain't a curse,
but this world.

Kikiope It doesn't matter now.

Kayode Y'know Mum an' Pastor knew each other?

Kikiope They did?

Kayode What if you were right?

Kikiope It doesn't matter.

Kayode Why not?

Kikiope Cos I fought, Kayode, thass why.
You all said I was wrong,
an I've conceded now
heeded all your words.

A woman stole you, Kayode,
the rain has drowned you
cos she cursed you
to sow no works,
no perks –

Kayode An' you believe that?

Kikiope Yes.

Kayode You don't.

Kikiope If it ain't a curse, then what is it?

Kayode I dunno.

Kikiope Kayode.

Kayode I dunno, Keeks.
Austerity?
Gentrification?
Livin in a place
we helped rebuild
but were never
allowed to build in
space for us?

Kikiope I ain't doin this.

Kayode S'that what Pastor told you to say?

Kikiope What?

Kayode S'this part of his plan?

Kikiope I ain't –
Kayode You still speakin to him?

Kikiope It was one visit.
You wanted me to be on his side.

Kayode Now I want you on mine.

–

Kikiope You should speak to Dr Davis.

Kayode No.

Kikiope Why not?
   If you, of all people, after all this,
   say Pastor Matanmi issa fraud,
   that there ain't no curse
   then let's go back.
   Go back an' pretend we had the bravery
   all those years ago.
   Let's be ruthless an' name it.

Kayode I dunno what –

Kikiope You're depressed, Kayode.

Kayode No.

Kikiope You're depressed.

Kayode (*scoffs*) I ain't de—
   S'this what Dr Davis is tellin you?

Kikiope No, I –
Kayode Cos she's been trained by the white man, y'know?
   Got you usin their words for somethin that ain't –

Kikiope I've known it for years.
   We both have, if we're honest.

Kayode You're wrong.
   I ain't.
   Thass what they might call it,
   but why we gotta label it like that?
   An' why're we just trustin em
   without –

Kikiope Cos that's what it is.
   We juss feared its meanin,
   then allowed your mum an' that man
   to shower us with tales of
   principalities an' powers
   towerin over your life.

77

–

Don't look at me like that.

Kayode I ain't dep . . .
  I ain't de . . .

Kikiope No?
  You think I've been tellin you to
  swim
  walk
  cycle
  for fun?
  Nah,
  it's cos I knew.
  An' if you don't care enough
  to admit it too,
  why should I?
  Why should I be on your side?

  Maybe I shouldn't.
  Cos I can't be held back, Kayode.
  The promotion was made official today –
  forty-seven K –
  but it's gonna mean more time away
  from home
  from you
  so I need you to speak.

  No.

  You juss sit there
  starin
  not bearin your soul.
  An' alas,
  I'm over it.

  Like you, I can't do these seven
  years
  all over again.

You see, your mum complains bout me
bein too 'British'
but prays against the witches an' wizards
of Lagos
against all ancestral spirits
against things sown by her forefathers,
but surely if she's so 'Nigerian'
then she should embrace that?

She's confused
an' that doesn't allow her to see clearly.

She would never acknowledge your depression.
It'd make her shook.
But you . . .
I expected more from you.
I expected truth.
I expected acknowledgement
rather than a burial.

We've discarded that for too long.
We haven't named it.
But we must.

–

Kayode's phone rings.

Kayode I should get this.

Kikiope Yeah.

He answers as Kikiope leaves,
and we hear the sound of rain.

As he speaks, Itan rises
like it's nothing,
like she was taking a nap.

He doesn't notice.

Kayode (*on phone*) Hello.
  Yes, speaking.

–

–

Oh, wow, that's . . .

–

Yes, of course.
  I'm gonna talk to my wife,
  but I'll call you back as soon as possible.

–

Of course.
  That's great, thank you.
  Speak soon.

> *He hangs up.*

Oh my gosh.

–

Keeks.

–

Kee—

> *Kikiope enters.*

Kikiope Yeah.

Kayode I juss got offered a job.

> *Her mouth drops in awe.*

Kikiope Thass . . .
Itan *rett muku tewn*

> *Kayode jumps at Itan's voice.*

80

Kikiope Well done.
Itan *zugaluma*

> *Itan and Kikiope embrace him.*

Kikiope We have to celebrate.

Itan Yaaas.

> *Kikiope goes to put on some music,*
> *but stops when she realises*
> *Kayode isn't happy.*

Kikiope Kayode, whass wrong?
  Is it bout what I said
  cos I was juss –

Kayode You're not the curse.

Kikiope What?
Itan I know.

Kikiope Kayode.

Kayode Who are you?
Kikiope Bout what I said . . .

Kayode Forget it.

Kikiope We can't –

Itan History.

Kayode Let's forget it.

Itan Agreed.

Kayode Let's juss be.

Kikiope Fine.

> *Itan leaves.*

I still think it'd be good to speak to Dr Davis.

Kayode Keeks.

Kikiope To help process the change.
   It might be a difficult transition.

Kayode I'll think bout it, but
   for now
   let's juss shut everythin out.
   Focus on us:
   husband an' wife,
   you an' I.
   Alright?

–

Y'hear that?
   It's rainin.

                          He plays 'By Your Side' by Sade.

Will you dance in the rain with me?

Kikiope I . . .
   Yeah.
   But I'm gonna put on
   a bonnet
   an' a raincoat
   this time.

Kayode (*laughs*) Cool.

                                  Kikiope heads out.

I'm gonna put on my –

                          *He tries to climb out of the ocean,
                                         but can't.*

I . . .

                          *He tries again, but can't.
                          Looks up in frustration.*

                          *He's about to burst, but
                          then looks at his reflection.*

He takes a deep breath.

Kayode, you can do it.
    You can do it.
    You can . . .

He reaches out of the ocean.
Begins to pull himself out.

It's not a quick or simple task.

Waves push him down.

But he fights them

with all his might

till he's on the shore.

Epilogue

Kayode and Kikiope's flat.
Kayode and Layo are together.

Itan is around, whistling
while packing his backpack.
He still eyes her with scepticism.

Layo Don't speak like that.
  You'll be great.

Kayode I'm rusty.

Layo They gave it to you for a reason.

Kayode Yeah.
  Pity.

Layo We both know that's not true.

–

I'm proud of you.

–

–

I'm thinking of moving back home.

Kayode What?
Layo It keeps calling me.

Kayode You can't go back.

Layo Why not?

Kayode Cos . . .
  What if you . . .

I mean,
you left for a reason.

Layo Yes, but I've overcome that now.

Kayode It doesn't linger?

Layo What do you mean?

Kayode Won't all the bad things come rushing back?

Layo They never left.

Kayode You can't pray it away then?

Layo We prayed the curse away
but it's more than that.
Hope enveloped me.
Desperation.
I wanted you to be free
and hoped that you could get rid of it all.
Not just the curse, but
all that my mistakes birthed in you . . .
This was never about a job for me.
I wanted you to have
victory.
I went from church to church
Desperate for that.
But maybe these discomforts are
meant to be
a part of
'the day of small things' –
which Zechariah describes –
ascribed to make you strong.

Kayode An' you think we're juss meant to accept it?
That we can still have peace
in the midst of it all?

Layo I don't have all the answers, Kayode.

–

–

Layo I should go.

Kayode We should –
Layo I didn't mean to stay this long.
   I just wanted to see you on your first day.

Kayode Thank you.

Kikiope enters.

Kikiope Oh, hello, Aunty.

Layo Hello, Kikiope.
Kikiope I thought I heard the door –

Layo I just came to say hello. How are you?

Kikiope I'm fine, thank you.

Layo Good.
Kikiope How are you?

Layo I'm well, Kikiope.
   I should get going to work.

Kikiope Wait, I got this book
   that our pastor recommended
   an' I bought you a copy.

Layo That's kind of you.
Kikiope It's juss in the room.

Layo Okay.
   Kayode, I'll see you later.

Kayode Yeah.
Layo Have a blessed day.

Kayode You too.

Kikiope and Layo leave.

Itan How does this feel, Kayode?
   Good?
   Do you feel complete now?

> Kayode doesn't answer,
> but his face does.
>
> He moves towards the ocean.
>
> Puts his hand in it.
> Strokes the water.
>
> Cries.
> For the first time.
>
> Kikiope enters.

Kikiope Hey, you ready to go?

> Itan holds up his backpack.

Kayode?

> He looks to Kikiope.
> Then to the water.
> Then ahead.
>
> Uncertain.
> Uneasy.
> Unfinished.
>
> The End.

Shukabhembemese to English Translations

TWO

uff un yi xemen yi missa eyle bret – where do you see yourself in five years?

utu grit pwe verne whuq un yi kivann zree – what type of work environment do you consider ideal?

FIVE

utu seeg yi unkana – what're you doing?

heynen reinn – stop this

y kivantar yi seegt rikana tieen pwe rei mernp – I thought you were getting rid of the curse

un yi kivann reinn vernet... heen – do you think this worked... no

yex quih udoj erfe – his plan will fall

heen – no

qleed – die

utu seeg yi unkana – what're you doing?

hinz frimn y – just join me

yerhy udoj moos bas ushung – we'll both be free

yi udoj xemen – you'll see

y puntu fylk giigra – I can fight hard

bas qlenza uxeb menna dallt ra y – be careful when it comes to me

heynen lemento yi mein – stop before you cry

yi udoj mein – you'll cry

y udoj vind menna yent wotlyneh – I'll make it my mission

y'oole mklena – I'm powerful

y udoj dall toogoo – I'll come back

giigraxuhn – harder

EIGHT

tili? – disappear

muku rett utu yi tantim padd – is that what you really want?

muku rett utu yi tantim iang yus – is that what you really desire?

un yerhy heent – don't we?

y crern yi – I love you

y akavi yi – you need me

la uume y niemm – so hold me close

agoun y crien – take me home

un heent vind y mein yii shimkana – don't make me cry by chanting

porzat ra lenke yee likkta – prayers to break our connection

reinn muku heent juplex – this isn't captivity

menna muku crern – it's love

topi puntuq yi – how could you?

yerhy seeg ashgen – we're family

TEN

tili jalaha – go away

heen – no

riksaw y – leave me

qleed – die

y'oole heina – I'm tired

masck y inkitar mklen numar ra fylk – but I have enough strength to fight

ELEVEN

rett muku tewn – that's amazing

zugaluma – well done

.